YEAR 9

Language Conventions

2011 edition
NAPLAN*- FORMAT PRACTICE TESTS
with answers

Essential preparation for Year 9
NAPLAN* Tests
Language Conventions

Don Robens

CORONEOS PUBLICATIONS

* These tests have been produced by Coroneos Publications independently of Australian governments and are not officially endorsed publications of the NAPLAN program.

YEAR 9 Language Conventions
NAPLAN*-FORMAT PRACTICE TESTS with answers
© Don Robens 2011
Published by Coroneos Publications 2011

ISBN 978-1-921565-97-7

* These tests have been produced by Coroneos Publications independently of Australian governments and are not officially endorsed publications of the NAPLAN program

THIS BOOK IS AVAILABLE FROM RECOGNISED BOOKSELLERS OR CONTACT:

Coroneos Publications
Telephone: (02) 9624 3977   Facsimile: (02) 9624 3717
Business Address: 6/195 Prospect Highway Seven Hills 2147
Postal Address: PO Box 2 Seven Hills 2147
Website: www.coroneos.com.au or www.basicskillsseries.com
E-mail: coroneospublications@westnet.com.au

Contents

NOTE:
- Students have 45 minutes to complete a test.
- Students must use 2B or HB pencils only.

The NAPLAN* Test

NAPLAN* is an acronym representing the National Assessment Program for Literacy and Numeracy. The tests are conducted in May each year to determine the Literacy and Numeracy skills of students in Australian schools. The results are then used by the authorities to benchmark schools on the distribution of these skills amongst students.

The tests are conducted in Year 3, Year 5, Year 7 and Year 9. The assessment program involves students completing four separate tests, in four timed minute sessions.

The separate tests are:

Writing: From 2011, students write a persuasive text in a 40 minute session. In previous years, students wrote a narrative.

Reading: Each student is given a 6 or 12 page stimulus book and completes a test comprising 35 to 40 plus multiple choice questions.

Language Conventions: This is a test of spelling, grammar and sentence structure.

Numeracy: This is a test consisting of multiple choice or short answer questions in numeracy (mathematics). In year 7 and Year 9 students answer non-calculator and calculator allowed questions in separate parts of the test.

This book is designed to help you practise for the NAPLAN* tests and develop the skills necessary to competently handle any task presented to you at this stage of your development.

* The practice tests in this book have been produced by Coroneos Pty Ltd independently of
  Australian governments and are not officially endorsed publications of the NAPLAN program

Language Conventions Test

The language conventions section of the test for year 9 consists generally of fifty-four questions where students are required to colour the bubble next to the correct answer from a choice of four.

The time allocated for the test is forty minutes and you will be required to use a 2B or HB pencil which is supplied specifically for the test.

It is important for the language conventions test that you remember that you are not being tested on new skills but things that you have already been taught in class. None of the questions are unknown or trying to trick you. The nature of the questions will vary with the common objective of testing the way language is used. Questions may include:

Grammar

Nouns, verbs, pronouns, adverbs, and other parts of speech should all be used correctly.

Tense

You may be given a sentence with a number of alternative suggestions on how to complete the sentence. Common mistakes in language occur when the writer uses past tense when the context of the sentence requires present or future tense.

Sentence Structure

Sentences should not contain too many ideas. The simple sentence has a subject, a verb and an object or predicate.

Spelling

Some examples include commonly misspelt words. The wrong spelling will be given, usually in the context of a sentence and you will be required to provide the correct spelling.

Vocabulary

Words and word meanings are commonly misunderstood.

Some examples of Language Conventions questions are...

The following questions contain one word which is spelt incorrectly. Write the correct word in the space provided.

1 The photoes were interesting.   **1** _____

2 It was a supprise.   **2** _____

3 The frute were ripe.   **3** _____

4 Check the calender.   **4** _____

The correct answers are   1 photos
                             2 surprise
                             3 fruit
                             4 calendar

5   **This sentence has one word that is incorrect.**

Write the correct spelling of the word in the box.

I herd a noise. ☐

To answer this you would write 'heard'.

6   **Which word correctly completes the sentence?**

The cars were _____ to the garage.

drive   drove   driven
 ○   ○   ○

The correct answer is driven.

Other questions may involve spelling, punctuation, sentences, missing words and completing sentences etc. You can revise by looking over what you have learnt in class and completing all the tests in this book.

LANGUAGE CONVENTIONS TEST 1

The spelling mistakes in these sentences have been underlined. Write the correct spelling for each underlined word on the line provided.

1   The secretery sat at the desk.

1 _____

2   The tomatos grew in the garden.

2 _____

3   A fashion catalog was on the table.

3 _____

4   Gymnasts were in the gymnaism.

4 _____

5   A commitee met in the library.

5 _____

6   The surgon operated on the patient.

6 _____

7   A musican practised for the performance.

7 _____

8   The choir rehersed in the hall.

8 _____

Read the text *Transport.* **The spelling mistakes have been underlined. Write the correct spelling for each underlined word in the box.**

Transport

The truck delivered the <u>parsel</u>.   **9**

The <u>traffick</u> had stopped moving.   **10**

Most vehicles used <u>petrolem</u> products.   **11**

Modern <u>feetures</u> were seen on the car.   **12**

Read the text *Libraries.* **The spelling mistakes have been underlined. Write the correct spelling for each underlined word in the box.**

Libraries

The <u>libarian</u> was busy.   **13**

The doors <u>openned</u> automatically.   **14**

<u>Dictonaries</u> were available for use.   **15**

It was a <u>magificient</u> library.   **16**

Each sentence has one word that is incorrect.
Write the correct spelling in the box.

17 The audiance clapped after the act.   **17**

18 It was an amatere act.   **18**

19 All were astonnished.   **19**

20 Aeraplanes flew to the airport.   **20**

Each sentence has one word that is incorrect.
Write the correct spelling of the word in the box.

21 The banannas were ripe.   **21**

22 A crowde watched the animals.   **22**

23 In the bin was an alluminium can.   **23**

24 It was an ambittios act to attempt.   **24**

25 Everyone read the advertisment.   **25**

26 The adresses were correct.   **26**

27 We were aloud to attend.   **27**

28 Many countrys competed.   **28**

29 A cow's stomah was full of grass.   **29**

30 They were good neegbours.   **30**

31 Which is the correct beginning for the sentence?

[   ] you heard the news?

Didn't   Don't   Haven't   Havn't
○   ○   ○   ○

32 Which sentence correctly uses italics?

○ On the *12 April* we finished reading the book.

○ The book's title was *Beautiful Space*.

○ *Parliament House* was in Canberra.

Shade one bubble

33 A stroke or slash (/) has been used in these sentences.

Which sentence is correct?

○ The map showed south/east Australia.

○ Mr/Mrs Jones were there.

○ The book was in black/white print.

34 Which word is missing?

[   ] the train arriving late people were happy to see it.

○ While

○ As

○ Although

○ Despite

35 Which sentence correctly uses brackets ( )?

○ The bus arrived early (we were glad).

○ The bus (for the excursion) arrived early.

○ The (excursion) bus arrived early.

36 Which pair of words correctly completes the sentence?

[   ] owns this book and [   ] book is this?

○ Whose   who

○ Who   whose

○ Who's   whose

37 What punctuation is missing from the end of the sentence?

Shade one bubble

In the zoo were bears, lions, birds, gorillas ▌

○ full stop (.)

○ question mark (?)

○ ellipsis points (...)

○ exclamation mark (!)

38 Which sentence is correct?

○ Neither the red or green matched.

○ Neither the red nor green matched.

○ Neither the red and green matched.

39 Where does the missing apostrophe (') go?

John's brothers shoes were on the doorstep.

40 Which sentence is punctuated correctly?

○ Sue asked, "Did you see the comet!"

○ Sue asked, "Did you see the comet."

○ Sue asked, "did you see the comet?"

○ Sue asked, "Did you see the comet?"

Read the text Space. Which words and punctuation correctly complete each sentence?

Space

Shade one bubble

In space **41** ⬜⬜⬜⬜ , moons, asteroids and comets are seen.
These may be observed through **42** ⬜⬜⬜⬜⬜⬜ .
43 ⬜⬜ a sight to be seen.

41 ◯ stars, planets

◯ stars and planets

◯ stars-planets

42 ◯ an observatory's telescope

◯ a observatory's telescope

◯ an observatorys' telescope

43 ◯ It's

◯ Its

◯ Their

Shade one bubble

44 Which words correctly complete the sentence?

The gorillas ▓▓▓ waiting – they knew they would be fed soon.

were	is	am	was
○	○	○	○

45 Which is the correct way to join the following sentences?
Jack read carefully. Jack thought. Jack then answered the question.

○ Jack read carefully, thought and then answered the question.

○ Jack read carefully, thinking and then answered the question.

○ Jack read carefully, jack thought, jack then answered the question.

46 Which sentence is correctly punctuated?

○ To buy apples, oranges and bananas; pay at the checkout.

○ To buy apples oranges and bananas pay at the checkout.

○ To buy apples, oranges and bananas, pay at the checkout.

47 Which word correctly completes the sentence?

▓▓▓ shop first and then go to the library.

I've	We'll	I'm	We're
○	○	○	○

48 Which words are all adverbs?

Shade one bubble

○ swim, dive, rest, walk

○ quickly, slowly, quietly

○ red, blue, happy, quiet

49 Which sentence is correct?

○ There's two new rooms in the school.

○ There was two new rooms in the school.

○ There is two new rooms in the school.

○ There're two new rooms in the school.

50 Which words correctly complete the sentence?

The fish swirled around the bait ▮▮▮▮▮▮ swallowed it.

so then   and so   and then

○   ○   ○

51 Which sentence has the correct punctuation?

○ "I'm finished!" indicated the man.

○ I'm finished!" indicated the man.

○ "I'm finished" indicated the man.

○ "I'm finished"! indicated the man.

52 Where do the two missing speech marks (" and ") go?

Shade two bubbles

○ ↓   ○ ↓   ○ ↓   ○ ↓

Sam asked, Are you okay, Mr. Thomas?

53 **Which of the following sentences have words with quotation marks around them (' and ') to tell the reader not to take them literally?**

Shade one bubble

⭕ The movie 'Sleeping Beauty' was a Disney movie.

⭕ The item was mistakenly advertised as a 'special'.

⭕ The movie was described as a 'good family movie'.

54 **Which words correctly complete this sentence?**

Over the bridge ▮▮▮▮▮▮▮▮▮▮ .

⭕ moved the traffic

⭕ move the traffic and pedestrians

⭕ moving the traffic

END OF LANGUAGE CONVENTIONS TEST 1

LANGUAGE CONVENTIONS TEST 2

The spelling mistakes in these sentences have been underlined. Write the correct spelling for each underlined word on the line provided.

1   Febuary is second month of the year.   1 _____

2   We did the test on Wedensday.   2 _____

3   A snake has a special tonge.   3 _____

4   The audience appladed the performer.   4 _____

5   We acomplished the task.   5 _____

6   It was a wonderful achevement.   6 _____

7   They apolagized for doing it.   7 _____

8   The animal's behaviour was intriging.   8 _____

Read the text Skeletons. The spelling mistakes have been underlined. Write the correct spelling for each underlined word in the box.

Skeletons

A skeleton is made up of many <u>peaces</u>.   **9**

It was a <u>genine</u> skeleton.   **10**

It was a <u>privelege</u> to see the skeleton's structure. **11**

The skeletons were in the <u>museem</u>.   **12**

Read the text Orchards. The spelling mistakes have been underlined. Write the correct spelling for each underlined word in the box.

Orchards

A <u>fotograph</u> of the orchard was taken   **13**

The orchardist <u>prefered</u> to grow apples.   **14**

<u>Unnecesery</u> spraying was eliminated.   **15**

The orchardist's <u>generousity</u> was often seen.   **16**

Each sentence has one word that is incorrect. Write the correct spelling in the box.

17 The programes were available now.   **17**

18 The show was recomended by many.   **18**

19 We went strait to the seats.   **19**

20 It was a challenging proceedure.   **20**

Each sentence has one word that is incorrect. Write the correct spelling of the word in the box.

21 The skin was swoollen.   **21**

22 There was suficent food for everyone.   **22**

23 A tiny caterpiller emerged from the egg.   **23**

24 No acommadation was available.   **24**

25 The theater was packed.   **25**

26 There were many theorees.   **26**

27 It was an embarasment.   **27**

28 Though the door we went.   **28**

29 That dimond is expensive.   **29**

30 It was a familar face.   **30**

31 Which is the correct beginning for the sentence?

Shade one bubble

_____ you hear the answer?

Didnt   Didn't   Haven't   Havn't

○   ○   ○   ○

32 Which sentence correctly uses italics?

○ The *Titanic* was sunk when it hit an iceberg.

○ We played the game in *March*.

○ The woman screamed *Help*!

33 A stroke or slash (/) has been used in these sentences.

Which sentence is correct?

○ There were blue/green/yellow colours in the picture.

○ They may/may not know the answer.

○ It will occur on Saturday/Sunday next weekend.

Shade one bubble

34 Which word is missing?

[   ] the library opened.

○ While

○ Next

○ Although

○ Unless

35 Which sentence correctly uses brackets ( )?

○ The driver (suddenly) stopped the car.

○ Suddenly he (the driver) stopped the car.

○ The driver stopped (the car).

36 Which pair of words correctly completes the sentence?

 borrowing this book and pen is this?

○ Whose   who

○ Who   whose

○ Who's   whose

37 What punctuation is missing from the end of the sentence?

Shade one bubble

The security guard called out, "Be careful ▮"

○ full stop (.)

○ question mark (?)

○ ellipsis points (...)

○ exclamation mark (!)

38 Which sentence is correct?

○ Harry was most impressed than the others.

○ Harry was the more impressed of all who saw it.

○ Harry was the most impressed of all who saw it.

39 Where does the missing apostrophe (') go?

○   ○   ○

Janes brother's books were on the shelf.

40 Which sentence is punctuated correctly?

○ "Did you see the garden!" asked Sally.

○ "Did you see the garden," asked Sally.

○ "did you see the garden?" asked Sally.

○ "Did you see the garden?" asked Sally.

Read the text *Vegetables*. Which words and punctuation correctly complete each sentence?

Vegetables

Shade one bubble

41 [   ] lettuces, carrots and cucumbers were growing in the garden. **42** [   ] watered each day. **43** [   ] nothing like a fresh vegetable to taste!

41 ○ Onions, tomatoes,

○ Onions tomatoes

○ Onions, tomatoes

42 ○ There

○ They're

○ They'll

43 ○ There's

○ There're

○ Theres

Shade one
bubble

44 **Which words correctly complete the sentence?**

The bus was travelling ▮▮▮ other buses.

next	along	behind	where
○	○	○	○

45 **Which is the correct way to join the following sentences?**

Jill knew the answer. Jill wrote the answer. Jill then checked it.

○ Jill knew the answer, wrote it and then checked it.

○ Jill knew the answer; wrote it; and then; checked it.

○ Jill knew the answer: wrote it and then checked it.

46 **Which sentence is correctly punctuated?**

○ We visited a museum, an aquarium and a beautiful garden.

○ We visited a museum an aquarium and a beautiful garden.

○ We visited a museum an aquarium, and, a beautiful garden

47 **Which word correctly completes the sentence?**

▮▮▮ the main actor.

There're	Theres	There's	Theirs
○	○	○	○

Shade one bubble

48 Which words are all adjectives?

○ swim, dive, rest, walk

○ quickly, slowly, quietly

○ red, blue, happy, quiet

49 Which sentence is correct?

○ Well be there soon.

○ We'll be there soon.

○ We're be there soon.

○ Where be there soon.

50 Which words correctly complete the sentence?

Around the corner travelled the car ▨▨▨▨ it was parked.

so then   and so   and then
○   ○   ○

51 Which sentence has the correct punctuation?

○ "Look!" called Dad. "we're here."

○ "Look!" called Dad. "We're here?"

○ "Look!" called Dad. "we're here."

○ "Look!" called Dad. "We're here!"

52 Where do the two missing speech marks
(" and ") go?

Shade two
bubbles

Are you feeling well? asked Mum.

53 Which of the following sentences have words with
quotation marks around them (' and ') to tell the
reader not to take them literally?

Shade one
bubble

○ What a 'joke' thought Jim.

○ The runner was 'out of sight'.

○ 'A stitch in time' will fix it.

54 Which words correctly complete this sentence?

The waves suddenly ⬛⬛⬛⬛⬛⬛ .

○ changed direction then

○ changed direction

○ changed direction suddenly

END OF LANGUAGE CONVENTIONS TEST 2

LANGUAGE CONVENTIONS TEST 3

The spelling mistakes in these sentences have been underlined. Write the correct spelling for each underlined word on the line provided.

1   The coin was surprisingly droped.   **1** _____

2   The goverment made the law.   **2** _____

3   A technology carreer was followed.   **3** _____

4   There was a scratch on his forhead.   **4** _____

5   We looked at the calender.   **5** _____

6   It had a three year garantee.   **6** _____

7   It was a permanant position   **7** _____

8   The animal's behavour was amazing.   **8** _____

Read the text *Energy.* **The spelling mistakes have been underlined. Write the correct spelling for each underlined word in the box.**

Energy

Hydroelectic power comes from water.　**9**

Renewabel energies are vital.　**10**

Electricity was genarated using wind.　**11**

Hydrogen batterys were often used.　**12**

Read the text Parliaments. The spelling mistakes have been underlined. Write the correct spelling for each underlined word in the box.

Parliaments

Many politicans were elected.　**13**

There were many electorats.　**14**

Electoneering continued for several weeks.　**15**

Politicians explaned their goals.　**16**

Each sentence has one word that is incorrect. Write the correct spelling in the box.

17	The driver used his driving license.	17	
18	The insect disapeared.	18	
19	He was a high jump champon.	19	
20	There was excitment in the air.	20	

Each sentence has one word that is incorrect. Write the correct spelling of the word in the box.

21	The dinning table was antique.	21	
22	There was a seperate place for that.	22	
23	The weather was changable.	23	
24	It was a marvelous day.	24	
25	The cheqee was presented to the man.	25	
26	It was a desparate situation.	26	

27 Lighting flashed during the storm.

27 ☐

28 Throo the ball at the target.

28 ☐

29 That the correct pronuncation.

29 ☐

30 It showed good managment.

30 ☐

31 **Which is the correct beginning for the sentence?**

▨ be a good reader.

Shade one bubble

Hed   he'd   He'd   He

○   ○   ○   ○

32 **Which sentence correctly uses italics?**

○ The saying is *'A bird in the hand is worth two in the bush'.*

○ We travelled over the *Sydney Harbour.*

○ The date was *3rd April.*

33 **A stroke or slash (/) has been used in these sentences. Which sentence is correct?**

○ First/second/third places were given medals.

○ They wrote yes/no to answer each question.

○ The car was travelling at 65/km/hr.

Shade one
bubble

34   Which word is missing?

[   ]   we were late the show had not yet started.

○ After

○ Next

○ Though

○ While

35   Which sentence correctly uses brackets ( )?

○ The plate (suddenly) dropped out of Dad's hands.

○ Suddenly he (Dad) dropped the plate.

○ He dropped the plate (Dad).

36   Which pair of words correctly completes the sentence?

[   ]   borrowing this book and   [   ]   need it for a week.

○ I'll   I've

○ I've   I'll

○ I'm   I'll

Shade one bubble

37 What punctuation is missing from the end of the sentence?

The lady questioned, "Do you know where to go ▮"

○ full stop (.)

○ question mark (?)

○ ellipsis points (…)

○ exclamation mark (!)

38 Which sentence is correct?

○ Barry payed for the clothes.

○ Barry pay for the clothes.

○ Barry paid for the clothes.

39 Where does the missing comma (,) go?

We counted one, two three and four before the game began.

40 Which sentence is punctuated correctly?

○ "Hello." called Tom. "can you hear me."

○ "Hello!" called Tom. "Can you hear me."

○ "Hello!" called Tom. "Can you hear me?"

○ "Hello," called Tom. "Can you hear me!"

Read the text Diseases. Which words and punctuation correctly complete each sentence?

Diseases

Shade one bubble

41 ▨ chicken pox... are diseases. They **42** ▨ fairly common even in our modern world. **43** ▨ some day these will be no more!

41 ○ Mumps, measles

○ Mumps measles

○ Mumps, measles,

42 ○ is

○ are

○ will

43 ○ May

○ Maybe

○ maybe

Shade one
bubble

44 **Which words correctly complete the sentence?**

The kangaroo was hopping ▢ the grass.

though   threw   through   thought
○   ○   ○   ○

45 **Which is the correct way to join the following sentences?**

Lightning flashed. Thunder rumbled. Rain fell.

○ Lightning flashed, thunder rumbled and rain fell.

○ Lightning flashed; thunder rumbled, and rain fell.

○ Lightning flashed and thunder rumbled and rain fell.

46 **Which sentence is correctly punctuated?**

○ "Did you see that? Its a snake! It's under that log!" stated Paul.

○ "Did you see that! It's a snake! It's under that log!" stated Paul.

○ "Did you see that? It's a snake! It's under that log!" stated Paul.

47 **Which word correctly completes the sentence?**

▢ the book you wanted.

Hears   Heres   Here's   Here
○   ○   ○   ○

48 **Which words are all verbs?**

○ swim, dive, rest, walk

○ quickly, slowly, quietly

○ red, blue, happy, quiet

Shade one
bubble

49 Which sentence is correct?

○ It's being too hours that we've waited here.

○ It's been two hours that we've weighted here.

○ Its been two hours that we've waited hear.

○ It's been two hours that we've waited here.

50 Which words correctly complete the sentence?

The blast shook the building causing ▮▮▮▮▮▮ collapse.

it too	it to	them to
○	○	○

51 Which sentence has the correct punctuation?

○ "Help? Who's there? Please help me!" yelled Max.

○ "Help! Who's there? Please help me!" yelled Max.

○ "Help. Who's there? Please help me!" yelled Max.

○ "Help! Who's there. Please help me!" yelled Max.

52 **Where do the two missing speech marks**

(" and ") go?

Shade two bubbles

Bob breathed deeply, lifted his head and shouted, I'm here!

---

53 **Which of the following sentences have words with**

quotation marks around them (' and ') to tell the

reader not to take them literally?

Shade one bubble

○ The 'Queen Elizabeth' ocean liner was in the harbour.

○ She was 'over the moon' when she heard the good news.

○ The story had a 'happy ending'.

---

54 **Which words correctly complete this sentence?**

The wind blew ▮▮▮▮▮▮▮▮▮ .

○ through that forest trees

○ through the forest

○ through those forest

END OF LANGUAGE CONVENTIONS TEST 3

LANGUAGE CONVENTIONS TEST 4

The spelling mistakes in these sentences have been underlined. Write the correct spelling for each underlined word on the line provided.

1 The <u>cylist</u> rode quickly.

1 _____

2 The <u>dictonery</u> was useful.

2 _____

3 He acted a funny <u>charactor</u>.

3 _____

4 We joined the <u>disussion</u> group.

4 _____

5 The <u>hieght</u> of the tree was about 10 m.

5 _____

6 The music had a catchy <u>rythm</u>.

6 _____

7 It had a <u>monotonus</u> beat.

7 _____

8 The story was <u>mysteryuos</u>.

8 _____

© Don Robens
Coroneos Publications

Read the text Sounds. The spelling mistakes have been underlined. Write the correct spelling for each underlined word in the box.

Sounds

They could <u>distingish</u> between the pitches. **9**

People were <u>unconscous</u> of some sounds. **10**

The singing showed <u>elegence</u>. **11**

A sound <u>gage</u> measured the sounds. **12**

Read the text Clothes. The spelling mistakes have been underlined. Write the correct spelling for each underlined word in the box.

Clothes

Many <u>vareties</u> were available to choose from. **13**

They were <u>skilfuly</u> made. **14**

Fashions were <u>changable</u>. **15**

A sales <u>representetive</u> talked with us. **16**

Each sentence has one word that is incorrect. Write the correct spelling in the box.

17	The sissors were sharp.	**17**	
18	It was a grammer test.	**18**	
19	The story had a wierd ending.	**19**	
20	It was a regretable situation.	**20**	

Each sentence has one word that is incorrect. Write the correct spelling of the word in the box.

21	The bed matress was clean and firm.	**21**	
22	The spider was poisonus.	**22**	
23	The king was annoited.	**23**	
24	It was a minature model.	**24**	
25	A huge propellar turned around.	**25**	
26	It was a mountainos area.	**26**	

27 The mosqito was a nuisance.   **27**

28 The speech was persasive.   **28**

29 Conditions were extreemly unusual.   **29**

30 Her judgment was accurate.   **30**

31 **Which is the correct beginning for the sentence?**

[   ] hoping to do well in the test.

Shade one bubble

I've   I'm   I'll   I

◯   ◯   ◯   ◯

32 **Which sentence correctly uses italics?**

◯ *Mr and Mrs Brown* visited us.

◯ The plant had the name tag: *Lincoln Rose.*

◯ The skin cancer was *malignant.*

33 **A stroke or slash (/) has been used in these sentences. Which sentence is correct?**

◯ The buses would arrive at 1.30/2.30.

◯ Buses/trains departed at the same time.

◯ The bus travelled in a south/west direction.

Shade one bubble

34 Which word is missing?

The river's source was ▨ spring water bubbled from the ground.

○ were

○ wear

○ where

○ well

35 Which sentence correctly uses brackets ( )?

○ The ($7.50) price was reasonable.

○ Mum (and) Dad attended the event.

○ It was a spectacular (though long) event.

36 Which pair of words correctly completes the sentence?

▨ attend the function and ▨ prepared well for it.

○ I'll   I've

○ I've   I'll

○ I'm   I've

37 What punctuation is missing from the end of the sentence?

The lady listed lettuce, tomato ▨ as sandwich fillings.

○ full stop (.)

○ question mark (?)

○ ellipsis points (…)

○ exclamation mark (!)

Shade one bubble

38 Which sentence is correct?

○ Tomorrow we attended the event.

○ Yesterday we attended the event.

○ In the future we attended the event.

39 Where does the missing colon (:) go?

There were several colours to choose from red, blue, green...

40 Which sentence is punctuated correctly?

○ "Harry." called Tim. "it's ready."

○ "Harry!" called Tim. "it's ready."

○ "Harry!" called Tim. "It's ready?"

○ "Harry!" called Tim. "It's ready!"

Read the text Nations. Which words and punctuation correctly complete each sentence?

Nations

Shade one bubble

41 [_____] China, the U.S.A…. are nations of the world. These nations **42** [_____] our world. **43** [_____] are part of our modern and ever-changing world.

41 ○ Australia, India,

○ Australia, India

○ Australia India,

42 ○ make out

○ make up

○ make us

43 ○ Each

○ All

○ Everyone

Shade one bubble

44 **Which words correctly complete the sentence?**

The tunnel went ▓▓▓ the mountain.

thought   throw   through   though
○   ○   ○   ○

45 **Which is the correct way to join the following sentences?**

The rocket was ready. The countdown began. It was launched.

○ The rocket was ready, the countdown began and it was launched.

○ The rocket was ready the countdown began and it was launched.

○ The rocket was ready, the countdown began; and it was launched.

46 **Which sentence is correctly punctuated?**

○ "Where is it? I have to find it!" muttered Peter.

○ "Where is it! I have to find it." muttered Peter!

○ "Where is it. I have to find it." muttered Peter.

47 **Which word correctly completes the sentence?**

▓▓▓ home was on a corner.

Their   Theres   There's   They're
○   ○   ○   ○

48 **Is the underlined word a noun, verb, adjective or adverb?**

The new car was parked under a <u>large</u>, eucalypt tree.

○ noun

○ verb

○ adjective

○ adverb

Shade one bubble

49 Which sentence is correct?

- ⬭ The road two the city was reopened after being closed for to long.
- ⬭ The road to the city was reopened after being closed for to long.
- ⬭ The road too the city was reopened after being closed for too long.
- ⬭ The road to the city was reopened after being closed for too long.

50 Which words correctly complete the sentence?

We watched the seagulls ________ lunch.

and eight	and ate	and eat
⬭	⬭	⬭

51 Which sentence has the correct punctuation?

- ⬭ "One! Two! Three eggs! Why did they break," asked Jack?
- ⬭ "One? Two? Three eggs! Why did they break!" asked Jack.
- ⬭ "One! Two! Three eggs! Why did they break!" asked Jack?
- ⬭ "One! Two! Three eggs! Why did they break?" asked Jack.

52 **Where do the two missing speech marks (" and ") go?**

Shade two bubbles

It's here! called Mark. They had been looking a long time for it.

53 **Which of the following sentences have words with quotation marks around them (' and ') to tell the reader not to take them literally?**

Shade one bubble

○ It was a 'tall' story.

○ Charles 'Chuck' Smith answered the phone.

○ 'Lord of the Rings' is an intriguing movie.

54 **Which words correctly complete this sentence?**

Everyone ▓▓▓▓▓ after the test was completed.

○ were pleased

○ was pleased

○ is pleased

END OF LANGUAGE CONVENTIONS TEST 4

LANGUAGE CONVENTIONS TEST 5

The spelling mistakes in these sentences have been underlined. Write the correct spelling for each underlined word on the line provided.

1 That is the <u>twelth</u>.   **1** _____

2 The <u>acident</u> was a tragedy.   **2** _____

3 <u>Sosiety</u> was continually changing.   **3** _____

4 The <u>choire</u> sang beautifully.   **4** _____

5 We <u>beleived</u> the facts when we heard them. **5** _____

6 <u>Enrollment</u> details were completed.   **6** _____

7 The <u>vehickle</u> was parked illegally.   **7** _____

8 It was a <u>familar</u> story.   **8** _____

Read the text *Roads*. The spelling mistakes have been underlined. Write the correct spelling for each underlined word in the box.

Roads

Drivers were <u>cautous</u> in wet weather.   **9**

Moterists were driving slowly in the rain.   **10**

<u>Experence</u> was necessary in wet weather.   **11**

The road was <u>circuler</u> at the intersection.   **12**

Read the text *Mirrors*. The spelling mistakes have been underlined. Write the correct spelling for each underlined word in the box.

Mirrors

Mirrors revealed <u>reflectons</u>.   **13**

Checking in a mirror was a <u>rootine</u>.   **14**

The <u>platipus</u> saw the mirror.   **15**

Their <u>curiocity</u> led to them using the mirror.   **16**

Each sentence has one word that is incorrect. Write the correct spelling in the box.

17 The nurse needed assistence.	**17**	
18 The doctor checked the patent.	**18**	
19 The medical check was thurough.	**19**	
20 "Breath deeply," requested the doctor.	**20**	

Each sentence has one word that is incorrect. Write the correct spelling of the word in the box.

21 They guest the answer.	**21**	
22 We wondered wether the answer was right.	**22**	
23 They coppied the drawing.	**23**	
24 The books were alltogether.	**24**	
25 The adresses were correct.	**25**	
26 Ninty apples were in the box.	**26**	

27 The eigth page was read carefully.

27

28 It was a large peice of bread.

28

29 It was an extravagent purchase.

29

30 The yacht sailed on the water.

30

---

31 Which is the correct beginning for the sentence?

Shade one bubble

⬛ be glad when the rain ceases.

We've   We're   We'll   We

◯   ◯   ◯   ◯

---

32 Which sentence correctly uses italics?

◯ We visited the *botanical gardens*.

◯ The book was *The Best Ever Story*.

◯ The fairy tale ended *happily ever after*.

33 **A stroke or slash (/) has been used in these sentences. Which sentence is correct?**

Shade one bubble

○ The letter was expected on either Tuesday/Wednesday.

○ The Browns/Jones were neighbours.

○ The letter/delivery date will be Tuesday/Wednesday.

34 **Which word is missing?**

We knew where to go and what to ▮▮▮ .

○ where

○ wear

○ were

○ ware

35 **Which sentence correctly uses brackets ( )?**

○ The train (The 909) left right on time.

○ Mum (and I) were on the train.

○ The train travelled for (three hours).

36 **Which pair of words correctly completes the sentence?**

We ▮▮▮ and decided to ▮▮▮ again later.

○ meet   met

○ meat   meet

○ met   meet

Shade one bubble

37   What punctuation is missing from the sentence?

"That's the answer ▋ " remarked Barry.

⬭ full stop (.)

⬭ ellipsis points (…)

⬭ question mark (?)

⬭ exclamation mark (!)

38   Which sentence is correct?

⬭ The sun was shining tomorrow.

⬭ The sun will be shining tomorrow.

⬭ The sun won't shine yesterday.

39   Where does the missing colon (:) go?

The menu includes Baked Fish, Roasted Chicken, Roast Beef…

⬆   ⬆   ⬆
⬭   ⬭   ⬭

40   Which sentence uses speech marks and punctuation correctly?

⬭ "Monday, Tuesday and Wednesday," answered Wendy.

⬭ "Monday, Tuesday and Wednesday, answered Wendy."

⬭ "Monday Tuesday and Wednesday," answered Wendy.

⬭ Monday, Tuesday and Wednesday, answered Wendy.

Read the text Outer Space. Which words and punctuation correctly complete each sentence?

Outer Space

Shade one bubble

41 ▨▨▨▨ comets... are seen in outer space. Giant

telescopes **42** ▨▨▨▨ remarkable photos of some of these. These

wonderful photos **43** ▨▨▨▨ the beauty in outer space.

41 ○ Stars, quasars,

○ Stars, quasars

○ Stars; quasars

42 ○ took

○ is taking

○ have taken

43 ○ shown

○ have shown

○ is showing

Shade one bubble

44 Which words correctly complete the sentence?

That was the ⬛ choice of the three options.

best	better	more better	most best
○	○	○	○

45 Which is the correct way to join the following sentences?

John warmed up. He positioned himself. He dived in.

○ John warmed up, positioned himself, and dived in

○ John warmed up positioned himself, and dived in.

○ John warmed up, positioned himself and dived in.

46 Which sentence is correctly punctuated?

○ "That's it!" stated Sue. "I'm sure that's it!"

○ "That's it! stated Sue. I'm sure that's it!"

○ "Thats it!" stated Sue. "Im sure that's it!"

47 Which word correctly completes the sentence?

⬛ the way to go now.

Thats	That's	that	thats
○	○	○	○

Shade one
bubble

48 Is the underlined word a noun, verb, adjective

or adverb?

The <u>muddy</u>, flooded river flowed out to sea.

○ noun

○ verb

○ adjective

○ adverb

49 Which sentence is correct?

○ The largest of the two elephants swam in the lead across the river.

○ The larger of the two elephants swam in the lead across the river.

○ The more larger of the two elephants swam in the lead across the river.

○ The most largest of the two elephants swam in the lead across the river.

50 Which words correctly complete the sentence?

We ate our lunch ▆▆▆▆▆▆ on a seat near the garden.

next to   while sitting   and sitting

○   ○   ○

51 Which sentence has the correct punctuation?

○ "One… two… three…. Three beautiful flowers" exclaimed Ruth.

○ "One… two… three….! Three beautiful flowers! exclaimed Ruth".

○ "One… two… three….! Three beautiful flowers" exclaimed Ruth

○ "One… two… three….! Three beautiful flowers!" exclaimed Ruth.

52 Where do the two missing speech marks (" and ") go?

Shade two bubbles

Christopher replied, This is what you need.

53 Which of the following sentences have words with quotation marks around them (' and ') to tell the reader not to take them literally?

Shade one bubble

○ The bird flew 'over the rainbow'.

○ The 'grass was greener' after the rain.

○ The address was '15 Rainbow Street, Colourville'.

54 Which words correctly complete this sentence?

The two students showed they ▮▮▮▮ in the topic.

○ are interested

○ is interested

○ am interested

END OF LANGUAGE CONVENTIONS TEST 5

LANGUAGE CONVENTIONS TEST 6

The spelling mistakes in these sentences have been underlined. Write the correct spelling for each underlined word on the line provided.

1   It is an <u>obediant</u> dog.   **1** _____

2   The <u>documentery</u> was worthwhile.   **2** _____

3   The <u>editer</u> worked late.   **3** _____

4   It was the <u>eassiest</u> way to go.   **4** _____

5   Their <u>enthusiesm</u> was obvious.   **5** _____

6   The <u>entreprenur</u> loved his work.   **6** _____

7   It was a <u>humorus</u> story.   **7** _____

8   It was a large <u>maintenence</u> job.   **8** _____

Read the text Gifts. The spelling mistakes have been underlined. Write the correct spelling for each underlined word in the box.

Gifts

It was a brilliant <u>manusript</u>.   **9**

They were <u>wraping</u> the gift.   **10**

The gift was a space <u>satelite</u>.   **11**

Tony was <u>persaded</u> to give the gift.   **12**

Read the text Imagination. The spelling mistakes have been underlined. Write the correct spelling for each underlined word in the box.

Imagination

It was an <u>imaginery</u> situation.   **13**

It involved giving <u>medacine</u>.   **14**

There was a <u>shiney</u> mirror.   **15**

Part of the story was <u>omited</u>.   **16**

Each sentence has one word that is incorrect. Write the correct spelling in the box.

17   Her pasttime was reading.   17 [   ]

18   The bird ate the biscute.   18 [   ]

19   The artical was written by Kate.   19 [   ]

20   The ship's ancor was heavy.   20 [   ]

Each sentence has one word that is incorrect. Write the correct spelling of the word in the box.

21   They were amatere tennis players.   21 [   ]

22   Paul's leg achhed after he fell over.   22 [   ]

23   It was an aereal photograph.   23 [   ]

24   The old coin was very valuabel.   24 [   ]

25   There were many sandwichs left over.   25 [   ]

26   Anne played the pianio well.   26 [   ]

27 Read that pamplet.

27

28 His muscels were sore.

28

29 He was a likable character.

29

30 That was the funiest story.

30

31 Which is the correct beginning for the sentence?

Shade one bubble

⬛ raining heavily.

It'll	It's	Its	It
○	○	○	○

32 Which sentence correctly uses italics?

○ The name of their home was *Mountain View*.

○ "I*'ll* do that task," said Michael.

○ The Olympic Games were a *total success*.

33 A stroke or slash (/) has been used in these sentences. Which sentence is correct?

Shade one bubble

○ The letter travelled / from city to country.

○ Mr/Mrs Kite were invited to the occasion.

○ We visited 4/77 Wren /Avenue.

34 Which word is missing?

We knew where ▮▮▮ been by checking the map.

○ where

○ we'd

○ we've

○ we're

35 Which sentence correctly uses brackets ( )?

○ The train (was red) left right on time.

○ Soxie (a Labrador) was a very intelligent dog.

○ It rained (heavily) during the night.

36 Which pair of words correctly completes the sentence?

I ▮▮▮ finished and ▮▮▮ now have a rest.

○ got   are

○ have   will

○ has   will

37 **What punctuation is missing from the sentence?**

After seeing bones, shells, ancient remains ▮ we left the museum.full

○ stop (.)

○ ellipsis points (…)

○ question mark (?)

○ exclamation mark (!)

38 **Which sentence is correct?**

○ Yesterday we are going to the venue.

○ Today we are going to the venue.

○ Yesterday we will going to the venue.

39 **Where does the missing comma (,) go?**

While at the farm we saw sheep cattle and horses.

40 **Which sentence uses speech marks (" and ") correctly?**

○ "Okay, let's go, agreed Tim and Ben."

○ "Okay," let's go, agreed Tim and Ben.

○ "Okay, let's go," agreed Tim and Ben.

○ "Okay, let's go, agreed," Tim and Ben.

Read the text Technology. Which words and punctuation correctly complete each sentence?

Shade one bubble

Technology

41 ▊▊▊▊▊ televisions… are instances of modern technology. Computers and phones in shops are **42** ▊▊▊▊▊ than those in museums. The fact they are constantly changing gives people choice and the option to access the **43** ▊▊▊▊▊ in technology.

41 ○ Computers, phones,

○ Computers, phones

○ Computers phones

42 ○ most modern

○ more modern

○ modern

43 ○ more latest

○ latest

○ most latest

Shade one bubble

44 **Which words correctly complete the sentence?**

We had to decide which was ▮▮▮ from the meat, chicken and fish meals.

best	better	more better	most best
○	○	○	○

45 **Which is the correct way to join the following sentences?**

Julie read the question. She thought. She then wrote her answer.

○ Julie read the question thought, and then wrote her answer.

○ Julie read the question thought and then wrote her answer.

○ Julie read the question, thought and then wrote her answer.

46 **Which sentence is correctly punctuated?**

○ "Its sunny!" exclaimed Jack. "That's great!"

○ "It's sunny!" exclaimed Jack. "That's great!"

○ "It's sunny!" exclaimed Jack. "Thats great!"

47 **Which word correctly completes the sentence?**

▮▮▮ the book you have been looking for.

Their's	There's	Theres'	Ther's
○	○	○	○

Shade one bubble

48 Is the underlined word a noun, verb, adjective or adverb?

A tiny bird <u>busily</u> built a small nest in the thick bush.

- ○ noun
- ○ verb
- ○ adjective
- ○ adverb

49 Which sentence is correct?

- ○ People choose either a apple or an orange.
- ○ People chose either a apple or a orange.
- ○ People chose either an apple or an orange.
- ○ People choose either an apple and an orange.

50 Which words correctly complete the sentence?

The students ______ into the library to research.

quietly moved	quitely moved	quietly moving
○	○	○

51 Which sentence has the correct punctuation?

- ○ "Ten, nine, eight… Blast off It's good" yelled the voice.
- ○ "Ten, nine, eight…! Blast off! It's good!" yelled the voice.
- ○ "Ten, nine, eight…! Blast off It's good!" yelled the voice
- ○ "Ten nine eight…! Blast off! It's good! yelled the voice.

Shade two bubbles

52 **Where do the two missing speech marks**

(" and ") go?

Peter thought and then said, That's the answer.

---

53 **Which of the following sentences have words with quotation marks around them (' and ') to tell the reader not to take them literally?**

Shade one bubble

○ The room was 'spick and span'.

○ There was a 'terrible' shark attack.

○ They had 'scrubbed up' for the occasion.

---

54 **Which words correctly complete this sentence?**

The two students showed they   in the topic.

○ were'nt interested

○ weren't interested

○ weren't interesting

END OF LANGUAGE CONVENTIONS TEST 6

ANSWERS

© Don Robens
Coroneos Publications

Year 9 Language Conventions
NAPLAN*-Format Practice Tests

TEST 1

1. secretary   **2**. tomatoes   **3**. catalogue   **4**. gymnasium   **5**. committee

6. surgeon   **7**. musician   **8**. rehearsed   **9**. parcel   **10**. traffic

11. petroleum   **12**. features   **13**. librarian   **14**. opened   **15**. Dictionaries

16. magnificent   **17**. audience   **18**. amateur   **19**. astonished

20. aeroplanes   **21**. bananas   **22**. crowd   **23**. aluminium   **24**. ambitious

25. advertisement   **26**. addresses   **27**. allowed   **28**. countries

29. stomach   **30**. neighbours   **31**. Haven't   **32**. … Beautiful Space.

33. Mr/Mrs Jones…   **34**. Despite   **35**. The bus (for the excursion) …

36. Who whose   **37**. ellipsis points (…)   **38**. Neither… nor…

39. … brother's…   **40**. Sue asked, "Did you see the comet?"

41. stars, planets   **42**. an observatory's telescope   **43**. It's   **44**. were

45. Jack read carefully, thought and then …   **46**. To buy apples, oranges
and bananas, pay at the checkout.   **47**. We'll   **48**. quickly, slowly, quietly

49. There're two …   **50**. and then   **51**. "I'm finished!" indicated the man.

52. Sam asked, "Are you okay, Mr Thomas?"   **53**. The item was mistakenly
advertised as a 'special'.   **54**. moved the traffic

TEST 2

1. February   **2**. Wednesday   **3**. tongue   **4**. applauded

5. accomplished   **6**. achievement   **7**. apologized or apologised

8. intriguing   **9**. pieces   **10**. genuine   **11**. privilege   **12**. museum

13. photograph   **14**. preferred   **15**. Unnecessary   **16**. generosity

17. programs   **18**. recommended   **19**. straight   **20**. procedure

21. swollen   **22**. sufficient   **23**. caterpillar   **24**. accommodation

25. theatre   **26**. theories   **27**. embarrassment   **28**. Through   **29**. diamond

30. familiar   **31**. Didn't   **32**. … Titanic....   **33**. They may/may not…

34. Next   **35**. Suddenly he (the driver)…   **36**. Who's whose

37. exclamation mark (!)   **38**. Harry was the most impressed…

39. Jane's…   **40**. "Did you see the garden?" asked Sally.   **41**. Onions,

tomatoes,   **42**. They're   **43**. There's   **44**. behind   **45**. Jill knew the answer,

wrote it and then checked it.   **46**. We visited a museum, an aquarium and a

beautiful garden.   **47**. There's   **48**. red, blue, happy, quiet   **49**. We'll be…

50. and then   **51**. "Look!" called Dad. "We're here!"   **52**. "Are you feeling

well?" asked Mum.   **53**. What a 'joke' thought Jim.

54.… changed direction.

TEST 3

1. dropped   **2**. government   **3**. career   **4**. forehead **5**. calendar

6. guarantee   **7**. permanent   **8**. behaviour   **9**. Hydroelectric

10. Renewable   **11**. generated   **12**. batteries   **13**. politicians

14. electorates   **15**. Electioneering   **16**. explained   **17**. licence

18. disappeared   **19**. champion   **20**. excitement   **21**. dining

22. separate   **23**. changeable   **24**. marvellous   **25**. cheque

26. desperate   **27**. Lightning   **28**. Throw   **29**. pronunciation

30. management   **31**. He'd   **32**. The saying is 'A bird … bush'.

33. They wrote…   **34**. Though   **35**. Suddenly he (Dad)…   **36**. I'm   I'll

37. question mark (?)   **38**. Barry paid…   **39**. … one, two…

40. "Hello!" called Tom. "Can you hear me?"   **41**. Mumps, measles,

42. are   **43**. Maybe   **44**. through   **45**. Lightning flashed, thunder

rumbled and rain fell.   **46**. "Did you see that? It's a snake! It's under that

log!" stated Paul.   **47**. Here's   **48**. swim, dive, rest, walk

49. It's been two hours that we've waited here.   **50**. it to

51. "Help! Who's there? Please help me!" yelled Max.   **52**. Bob… shouted,

"I'm here!"   **53**. She was 'over the moon' ….   **54**. through the forest

TEST 4

1. cyclist   2. dictionary   3. character   4. discussion   5. height

6. rhythm   7. monotonous   8. mysterious   9. distinguish

10. unconscious   11. elegance   12. gauge   13. varieties   14. skilfully

15. changeable   16. representative   17. scissors   18. grammar

19. weird   20. regrettable   21. mattress   22. poisonous   23. anointed

24. miniature   25. propeller   26. mountainous   27. mosquito

28. persuasive   29. extremely   30. judgement   31. I'm   32. The plant had
a name tag: Lincoln Rose.   33. Buses/trains.   34. where

35. It was a spectacular (though long) event.   36. I'll   I've

37. ellipsis points (…)   38. Yesterday…   39. … choose from: red…

40. "Harry!" called Tim. "It's ready!"   41. Australia, India,   42. make up

43. All   44. through   45. The rocket was ready, the countdown began and it
was launched.   46. "Where is it? I have to find it!" muttered Peter.

47. Their   48. adjective   49. The road to the city was reopened after being
closed for too long.   50. and ate   51. "One! Two! Three eggs! Why did they
break?" asked Jack.   52. "It's here!" called Mark…   53. It was a 'tall' story.

54. was pleased

TEST 5

1. twelfth   **2**. accident   **3**. Society   **4**. choir   **5**. believed   **6**. Enrolment

7. vehicle   **8**. familiar   **9**. cautious   **10**. Motorists   **11**. Experience

12. circular   **13**. reflections   **14**. routine   **15**. platypus   **16**. curiosity

17. assistance **18**. patient   **19**. thorough   **20**. Breathe   **21**. guessed

22. whether   **23**. copied   **24**. altogether   **25**. addresses   **26**. Ninety

27. eighth   **28**. piece   **29**. extravagant   **30**. yacht   **31**. We'll

32. The book was *The Best Ever Story.*   **33**. The Browns/Jones were …

34. wear   **35**. The train (The 909) left right on time.   **36**. met   meet

37. exclamation mark (!)   **38**. The sun will be shining tomorrow

39. The menu includes: **40**. "Monday, Tuesday and Wednesday," answered

Wendy.   **41**. Stars, quasars,   **42**. have taken   **43**. have shown   **44**. best

45. John warmed up, positioned himself and dived in.   **46**. "That's it!" stated

Sue. "I'm sure that's it!"   **47**. That's   **48**. adjective   **49**. The larger…

50. while sitting   **51**. "One… two… three…! Three beautiful flowers!"

exclaimed Ruth.   **52**. Christopher replied, "This… need."   **53**. The bird flew

'over the rainbow'.   **54**. are interested

TEST 6

1. obedient   **2**. documentary   **3**. editor   **4**. easiest   **5**. enthusiasm

6. entrepreneur   **7**. humorous   **8**. maintenance   **9**. manuscript

10. wrapping   **11**. satellite   **12**. persuaded   **13**. imaginary

14. medicine   **15**.shiny   **16**. omitted   **17**. pastime   **18**. biscuit

19. article   **20**. anchor   **21**. amateur   **22**. ached   **23**. aerial   **24**. valuable

25. sandwiches   **26**. piano   **27**. pamphlet   **28**. muscles   **29**. likeable

30. funniest   **31**. It's   **32**. The name of the home was *Mountain View.*

33. Mr/Mrs Kite...   **34**. we'd   **35**. Soxie (a Labrador)...   **36**. have   will

37. ellipsis points (...) **38**. Today we are going to the venue.   **39**. ...sheep,

cattle...   **40**. "Okay, let's go," agreed Tim and Ben. **41**. Computers, phones,

42. more modern   **43**. latest   **44**. best   **45**. Julie read the question,

thought and then wrote her answer. **46**. "It's sunny!" exclaimed Jack. "That's

great!"   **47**. There's   **48**. adverb   **49**. People chose either an apple or an

orange.   **50**. The students quietly moved into...   **51**. "Ten, nine, eight...!

Blast off! It's good!" yelled the voice.   **52**. Peter thought and then said,

"That's the answer."   **53**. They had 'scrubbed up' for the occasion.

54. weren't interested

Year 9 Language Conventions
NAPLAN*-Format Practice Tests